Let's Start!
SCIENCE

Hear this!

Sally Hewitt

QED Publishing

First published in the UK in 2005 by
QED Publishing
A Quarto Group company
226 City Road
London EC1V 2TT

www.qed-publishing.co.uk

A Catalogue record for this book is available
from the British Library.

ISBN 1 84538 166 1

Written by Sally Hewitt

Project Editor: Honor Head
Series designer: Zeta Jones
Photographer: Michael Wicks
Picture Researcher: Nic Dean
Series Consultant: Sally Morgan

Publisher Steve Evans
Creative Director Louise Morley
Editorial Manager Jean Coppendale

Printed and bound in China

The words in bold
like this are
explained in the
Glossary on page 22.

Contents

Hear this

You have five senses that give you all kinds of information about what is going on around you.

The five senses are sight, touch, taste, smell and **hearing**.

This book is about hearing.

◀ Your sense of hearing helps you to understand what people say.

Some sounds warn you of danger. A speeding emergency vehicle has a **loud** siren. It means

Take care! Keep out of the way!

Music is a sound that you can enjoy. Do you like listening to music?

What other sounds do you like to hear?

Listen!

The world around you is full of sounds. What can you hear now?

▲ Your **ears** are the part of your body you use to hear.

Listen! Can you hear any sounds you have never heard before?

You can hear air moving inside a shell. Does it sound like the sea?

You sometimes know what is happening around you by listening to the noises.

Ask a friend to shut their eyes and listen while you:

- bounce a ball
- pour milk into a glass
- tear a piece of paper
- bite an apple

Can your friend tell you what you are doing by the sounds you make?

Sound waves

You can hear the sound of helicopter blades turning.

The blades move the air around them and make **sound waves**.

You can't see sound waves but you can hear them.

A bird singing makes a different pattern of sound waves.

You hear when sound waves go into your ears. Your ears send a message to your brain. Your brain tells you what you are hearing.

Where's that sound?

Your ears are small and flat. You have to turn your head to move them.

◀ Cup your hand around your ear and point it towards a sound. Does it sound louder now?

Different animals have differently shaped ears. Some animals can hear better than you.

▶ This dog can turn its ears towards a sound without moving its head.

You have two ears to help you find out where a sound is coming from. You can usually tell where someone is by listening to the sounds they make.

Ask a friend to shut his or her eyes. Tiptoe around them, then stop and make a tiny squeak.

Can your friend point to where you are just by listening?

Eardrums

outer ear

eardrum

Your **eardrum** is a small piece of skin inside your ear. It is stretched tightly like a drum skin.

When you bang a drum, the skin **vibrates**. This means it pushes the air around it backwards and forwards.

When a sound goes into your ears, it hits your eardrum and makes it vibrate.

Make your own sound waves.
- Stretch some cling film over a bowl. (This is like your eardrum.)
- Sprinkle rice on top.
- Bang a baking tray with a wooden spoon just above it.
- Watch the sound waves vibrate the cling film and make the rice jump.

Loud and quiet

Loud sounds make very large vibrations in the air. They can hurt your ears!

You can put your hands over your ears to keep out some of the sound.

A dog barking is a loud sound. What other loud sounds have you heard?

Quiet sounds make small vibrations.
You have to listen carefully to hear them.

You can hear **quiet** sounds better when
they are close to your ear.

Whispering is a quiet sound.
What other quiet sounds
have you
heard?

Near and far

A car engine sounds loud when you are near it. The sound becomes quieter and quieter as the car moves further away.

As sound travels through the air, it spreads out and becomes quieter.

Your voice can travel along string into your friend's ear.

- Make a hole in the bottom of two plastic cups.
- Thread a long piece of string through each hole.
- Fix the string with buttons.
- Give a cup to a friend and pull the string tight.
- Talk into one cup. Your friend will hear your voice through the cup at the other end.

High and low

Musical instruments play **high** and **low** notes.

The thick strings on a guitar play low notes.

The thin strings on a guitar play higher notes.

◀ The strings on a guitar play different notes.

You can play high
and low notes on
a glass of water.

- Pour yourself a glass of water or juice.
- Tap the glass gently with a spoon
  and listen to the sound.
- Have a drink. Tap the
  glass again.
- How has the sound
  changed?
- Tap every time you
  have a drink.

Does the note get
higher or lower?

I can't hear

People who can't hear can learn to tell what someone is saying by watching their face and lips.

Some deaf people can make signs with their hands to talk to each other. This is called sign language.

These children are saying 'hello' in sign language.

You can mime, or make movements, to tell a story without speaking.

What story could this boy be telling?

Can you tell a story without saying a word?

Glossary

Eardrum

A small piece of skin inside your ear like a drum skin.

Ears

You have two ears. They are the parts of your body you hear with.

Hearing

Hearing is one of your five senses. You hear with your ears.

High

Sounds can be high. A bird singing makes a high sound.

Loud

Sounds can be loud. A road drill makes a loud sound.

Low

Sounds can be low. A dog growling makes a low sound.

Quiet

Sounds can be quiet. Whispering is a quiet sound.

Sound waves

Sounds travel through the air in waves called sound waves.

Vibrate

To move backwards and forwards a tiny amount very fast.

Index

23

Parents' and teachers' notes

• Find words about sound throughout the book such as loud, quiet, high and low. Listen to different sounds. Talk about the sounds you hear using these words.

• Make a tape of everyday sounds, and use them to play 'What's That Sound?' Find new words to talk about the sounds such as splash, squeak, bang, patter and scrape.

• You can feel vibrations. Show your child how to put his or her hand on the speaker of a radio or CD player to feel the vibrations as the sound comes through.

• Make a big cardboard cone and use it like an ear trumpet. Put the end of the cone around, but not in, your child's ear. Point the ear trumpet towards a quiet sound. Does it make the sound louder?

• Cut out pictures of animals. Discuss the different sounds they make.

• Find pictures of things that make a noise, such as a leaf falling, a watch ticking, people whispering, someone shouting, a train, thunder, a jet taking off and a space rocket. Ask your child to put them in order, starting with the quietest sound.

• Look at pages 12–13. Talk about why loud noises, such as shouting, screaming, banging and drilling, can hurt your ears. Find out which workers protect their ears from loud noise when they work.

• When you walk along a busy street, discuss the sounds of the traffic. Which are the loudest vehicles? Which are the quietest? Notice how the sound of traffic gets louder as it approaches and quieter as it drives away.

• Ask your child to draw a picture of their face smiling surrounded by pictures of sounds they like. They can draw another picture of their face frowning surrounded by pictures of sounds they don't like. Talk about why they like some sounds and dislike others.

• Collect small pots with lids. Put rice, dried pasta, beans and coins in the pots. Shake the pots and listen to the different sounds they make.

• Look at pictures of different places such as the seaside, an airport or a farm. Talk about the sounds you might hear at these places.